# The First Book of Swimming

# The FIRST BOOK of
# SWIMMING

by DON SCHIFFER

Pictures by Julio Granda

## FRANKLIN WATTS, INC.
575 LEXINGTON AVENUE • NEW YORK 22

FIRST PRINTING

*Library of Congress Catalog Card Number: 60-11174*

© Copyright 1960 by Franklin Watts, Inc.

Printed in the United States of America
by Polygraphic Company of America, Inc.

# Contents

| | |
|---|---|
| Everyone Can Learn to Swim | 1 |
| First Learn the Safety Rules | 2 |
| One Step at a Time | 4 |
| Meet the Water | 5 |
| The Four Steps to Swimming | 6 |
| Treading Water Is Easy | 17 |
| The Dog Paddle — a Simple Stroke | 18 |
| The Crawl Stroke | 20 |
| The Backstroke | 30 |
| The Racing Backstroke | 33 |
| The Breaststroke | 34 |
| The Sidestroke | 36 |
| The Butterfly Stroke | 39 |
| Now You Must Practice | 40 |
| Simple Diving | 42 |
| The Racing Dive | 48 |
| Why Not Be a Racing Swimmer? | 50 |
| How a Swimming Meet Is Run | 54 |
| The Events in a Swimming Meet | 56 |
| How to Score a Meet | 60 |
| A Final Word | 61 |
| Index | 63 |

# Everyone Can Learn to Swim

SWIMMING is a healthful and rewarding sport. It provides as much fun and exercise for young people as it does for grownups. And anyone can learn — some babies have been taught to swim before they were one year old!

If you don't know how to swim, then now is the time to start learning. And even if you already swim, you can always learn to be a better, more proficient swimmer with added practice.

The best way to learn is through personal instruction. Many communities have learn-to-swim programs where instruction is given by experts. You can easily obtain information about these classes — where and when they are held, and how you can join them. If you do join such a class, you can use this book as a study aid at home.

If a learn-to-swim program is not available in your community, or if you don't want to wait until one is held, then you can learn by carefully following the instructions in this book. But there is one rule in learning to swim that you must never break: *Always have someone with you when you take a lesson.* This person must know how to swim so that he can help you practice and correct anything you are doing wrong.

This book is divided into three main parts. The first tells you about the fundamentals of swimming — such things as water safety, breath control, kicking, and floating. The second will tell about the different strokes — that is, the ways of moving yourself through the water. The third discusses swimming in organized racing.

1

# First Learn the Safety Rules

ONE REASON a child is taught to swim is for his own protection in the water. But even an expert swimmer is not safe in the water unless he follows the common rules of water safety. They are:

1. Never enter the water alone. Always have someone with you.

2. Wait at least one hour after eating before entering the water.

3. Never go swimming during a thunderstorm. If one should start while you are swimming, leave the water immediately.

4. Never go swimming when you are not feeling well.

5. Don't go swimming immediately after any violent exercise. Your overheated muscles may cramp in the water.

6. Know your limits as a swimmer. Don't "show off" in the water or get too far out from land.

7. Always obey the lifeguards who are stationed for your protection at ocean beaches, lakes, and pools.

8. Don't fool around in the water. This means no wrestling and no dunking your friends under the water.

9. Leave the water if you begin to feel chilly.

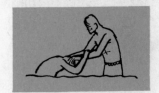

10. If you get into trouble in the water, call for help. When it comes, relax and follow the instructions of your rescuer.

# One Step at a Time

How did you learn to walk as a baby? First you sat up, then you crawled on the floor, then you stood up, and finally took a few steps holding on to the furniture or your mother's hand. Finally you were able to walk on your own: a few short steps at first, but soon you were running all over the house.

You will learn to swim the same way, one step at a time. Swimming is almost as natural as walking and once you learn you will never forget.

The best place to learn is in a regular swimming pool. The firm, even bottom of a pool, the depth of the water marked on its sides, and the clear water through which the underwater motions of other swimmers can be seen, all help the beginner.

But if there is no pool in your community, then a lake or a pond will do. Before you try learning in a lake or a pond, however, be sure there are no hidden rocks, tree stumps, or sharp objects under the surface, and that the bottom is firm — not muddy. Don't try to learn at ocean beaches — the water is often much too rough. Always observe Rule Number 1 when practicing in a lake or a pond: *Have someone with you.*

# Meet the Water

ONCE in your swimming suit, it's time to get acquainted with the water. Enter gradually until the water comes up to your waist. Walk around slowly, letting your arms trail through the water.

Now drop down in the water until it covers your shoulders, stretch out your arms and move them backward and forward. Notice that the backward pull of your arms will move your body forward.

Pick up some water in your cupped hands and spill it over your head. This first time in the water should be nothing but playing, that is, getting the "feel" of water all around your body. When you are completely at home in the water, it is time to begin your lessons — and not till then.

You are the one who must decide how much time to spend with each step that follows. You may be able to learn several steps in one lesson, or, perhaps you may have to study one step of a lesson several times. The time you take doesn't matter. It is best to learn each step *well* before going on to the next. Remember, what you learn now will last you for the rest of your life. On each trip to the pool or lake think about what you have already learned before going on to a new step.

# The Four Steps to Swimming

THERE ARE four major steps a beginner must learn in order to become a swimmer. They are: 1. Breath control; 2. Floating; 3. Kicking; 4. Stroking. The steps are usually taught in that order.

*How to control your breathing*

Whenever you see a good swimmer, watch him. If he is lying face down in the water, you will notice that his mouth is underwater much of the time. On every *other* stroke he will lift his mouth out of the water to breathe.

This ability to breathe rhythmically while swimming is called *breath control*. Since your face will be underwater much of the time when swimming, you can see how important it is to control your breathing so that you will take a breath only while your mouth is out of water.

Notice, we said *mouth*, not nose. Normally you breathe in and breathe out through your nose. But in swimming all breathing should be done through the mouth. Otherwise you might not get enough air each time you take a breath.

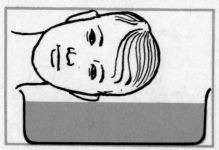 

6

The first step in learning breath control can be practiced with a basin of water. You should have about six inches of water in the basin — enough so that your nose won't strike bottom when you put your face under.

Put one cheek and ear against the top of the water. Take a breath through your mouth, then close your eyes and turn your head so your face is underwater. Now breathe out through your mouth.

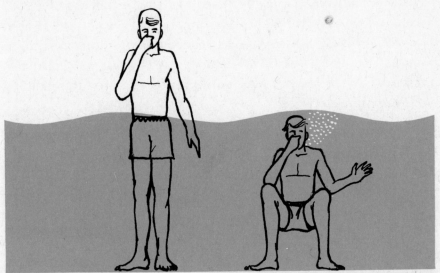

When you think you are ready, go into waist-deep water and do the same thing, while bending over. Keep your face under for a count of *five*, then turn your face and let your breath out. Take another breath and put your face under again, this time counting to *six*. Repeat this four more times, adding one count each time, until you can hold your breath underwater to the count of ten. Between each dunking, rest for a few seconds.

Now lower your body in the water until you are covered up to your chin. Take a deep breath, close your mouth tight, hold your nose, shut your eyes, and then lower your head under the water.

Stay under for a count of five, holding your breath.

Now try the same thing without pinching your nose and with your eyes open, but still holding your breath. As soon as your head is underwater open your eyes, put your fingers in front of your face and count them all before you come up.

After a few tries at this, go down again, and this time let your breath out slowly through your mouth while still underwater. Notice the bubbles of air rising to the surface. Come up again as soon as you finish exhaling (letting your breath out). Do this exercise as much as you like; until you feel comfortable holding your breath underwater.

Put a stick of wood or a toy boat on the water and see how it floats. Then hold it below the surface, let it go, and see how it jumps up to the surface again. The force which holds it up is called *buoyancy* and this same force will support your body in the water.

On dry land, or beside the pool, lie down flat, face down, arms straight up over your head and legs fully extended. Your body should be one straight line from the tips of your fingers to the tips of your pointed toes. Muscles should be relaxed. You are now in the position of the *prone* float.

Now roll over on your back. Keep the legs extended and close together, but separate your arms so that they point out at an angle halfway between head and shoulders. Keep the chin tucked against the chest. You are now in the position of the *back* float.

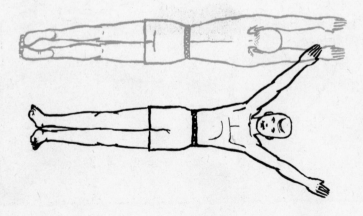

Enter the water to a spot about knee-high, where you have something to hold on to — either the side of the pool or the hands of a friend. Lean forward until your arms and chest are lying on the surface of the water (but keep your head up and out of the water). Now shove off from the bottom with your feet — they will rise to the surface just as the toy boat did. When you feel ready, take a deep breath, lower your face under the water then exhale and bring the head up again.

After you have tried the prone float this way until you feel perfectly comfortable doing it, then it is time to try it on your own, and in waist-deep water. Start the same way, leaning forward, but this time without holding on to anything. Take a deep breath and

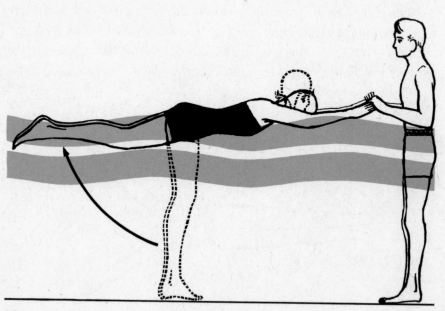

when you push off with your legs, give a good shove so that you will float forward, face down under the surface until you exhale. Then raise your head and stand up again.

To stand up from the prone float, pull your knees up under your body, push down through the water with your hands, raise your head sharply, and shove your legs down to the bottom. While doing this, your friend should be right by your side to help you, if you need him.

The only difference between the prone float and the back float is that in the back float you don't have to think about your face being under the water. Otherwise, it is very much the same.

Now find a place where the water just comes up to your neck

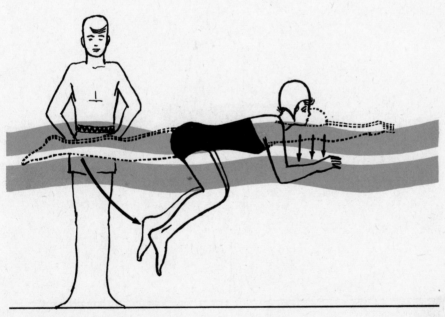

when you are sitting down. While you are sitting, put your hands on the bottom behind you. Then put your weight on your hands and push your legs off the bottom so that they rise to the surface. Let your head go back as far as you can. This will give you a good idea of what the back float is like.

Next, still in waist-deep water, have your friend stand behind you. Lean back while your friend supports your shoulders and guides your head and back down onto the water. When you are flat on the water, he can support your head for a while, then have him let go and move his hands down to support your hips and

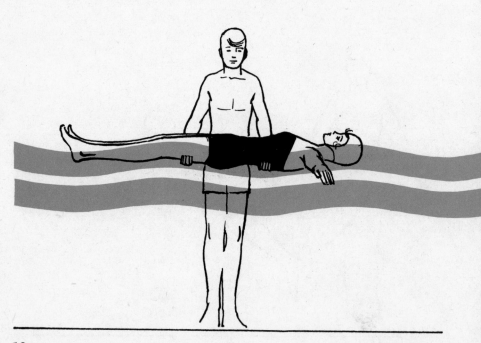

legs — because sometimes they sag beneath the surface. Finally, your friend should step aside and let you float completely free.

Practice the back float until you are able to keep your arms at your sides while you are flat in the water, then move them back to the position described above. If you are not able to keep your position with your arms above your head, bring them back to your sides and move them up and down slowly to help keep your body afloat.

To stand up from the back float, first let your hips drop in the water. Draw your knees up to your stomach, force your hands up hard against the water, and shove your legs downward. Use your hands and arms for balance. On the first few tries you will probably need your friend's help.

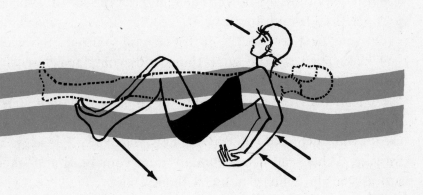

The major job of swimming is done by the hands and arms, but the legs also play their part by kicking. Just as there are several arm strokes used in swimming, there are also several leg strokes. The one you will learn first is the most common, and it is called the *flutter* kick. Later, you will learn other kicks.

Go into the prone float position, holding on to the pool side or your friend's hands. Keep your head above the water. Allow your feet to drop about a foot below the surface. Stay relaxed. Move your right leg up to the surface, then let it drop while you lift your left leg.

The legs are moved from hips to toes in one motion, but with knees slightly bent. The power of the kick comes from the foot. Kick slowly at first to get the rhythm: right leg up, left leg down — left leg up, right leg down. Then increase the speed. When your legs get tired, stand up and rest.

On your next try, have your friend pull you over the water as you kick. Then try the same thing with your face down in the water, holding your breath.

On later tries, tell your friend to let go before you put your face down under the water, but keep your arms extended. Now you are on your own, and you can feel how your kicking legs push you forward. When you need a breath, raise your head and stand up just as you did when floating without a kick.

When you feel you have fully mastered the flutter kick from the prone float, try it from the back float. Follow the same procedure you did from the prone float. Have your friend support your head

14

on the first few tries, then do it on your own. You have no breathing problem now, for your mouth stays out of the water at all times.

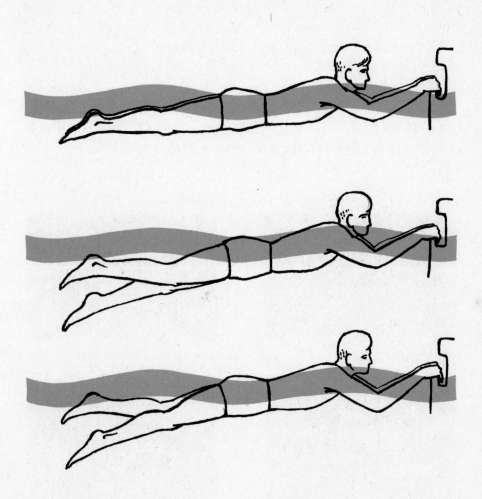

There are more than a half-dozen swimming strokes, but all of them are based on something you learned when you first stepped into the water: your arms and hands pushing through the water will move your body.

If your hands pull back through the water, your body moves forward; if your hands push forward, your body moves back. If your hands push down through the water, your body rises; if your hands pull up through the water, your body sinks.

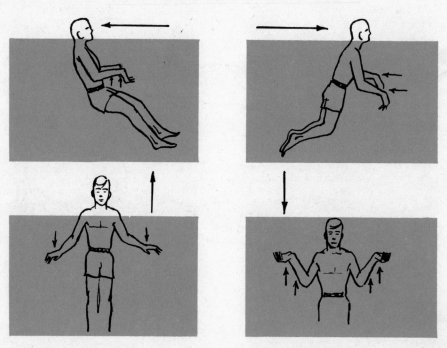

# Treading Water Is Easy

LET'S take that part about your hands pushing down through the water and see how it works out in practice. There is a trick in swimming known as "treading water." It keeps a swimmer afloat in deep water while his body remains in an upright position.

Find a place where the water is up to your chest. Now extend your arms sideward, just under the surface. Take your feet off the bottom and move your arms — first one and then the other — up and down slowly under the water. Your legs should pump slowly up and down, as if you were riding a bicycle. Keep your body relaxed. You will be surprised to find that treading water will keep your head above the surface with very little effort.

# The Dog Paddle — a Simple Stroke

FROM treading water, it is a natural step to your first swimming stroke — the *dog paddle*. Have you ever seen a dog in the water? If you have, you know where this stroke got its name. A dog uses his front paws to keep his head above water and his rear paws to push him forward. The dog's front paws sometimes break a bit above the surface, but his rear ones stay under at all times.

When you try the dog paddle, start from the position of treading water. Then lean forward and bring your hands up in front of your chest. Pull your right leg forward, bending it at the knee. As the right leg shoves back again, your left hand pulls down through the water.

Next, the left leg is brought up at the knee and shoved down again, the right hand going down with it as the left hand comes back to the chest. So it goes: right leg and left hand, left leg and right hand.

The body position in the dog paddle is about halfway between a prone float and the upright float. The head stays above the water at all times, and the strokes bring only part of your hand out of the water. The motion of the arms, as the elbows are bent, is a small circle; starting at the chest, going out, down through the water and back to chest height; then out, down again, and so on. Also, the fingers of the hand should be cupped, sending more water behind you and thus making you go faster.

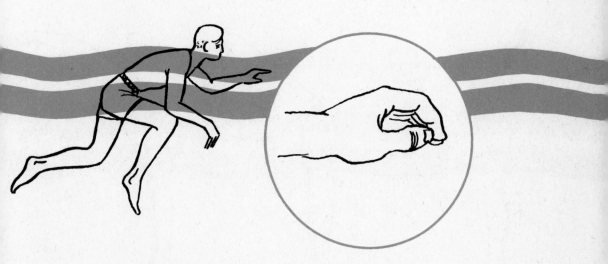

# The Crawl Stroke

FROM the slowest of swimming strokes, we move now to the fastest — the *crawl*. Strange name for a fast stroke, isn't it? The crawl is the stroke most frequently used in swimming both for fun and in racing. To perform it correctly you must learn to breathe, kick, and stroke at the same time.

Since the crawl is the most important stroke, we will break it up into six parts and learn it one part at a time. You will take this first lesson standing on the land.

1. Stand, as relaxed as possible, with your feet about fifteen inches apart, and bend forward from the waist. Let both arms hang straight down from the shoulder. Your fingers will be separated if your arms are relaxed.

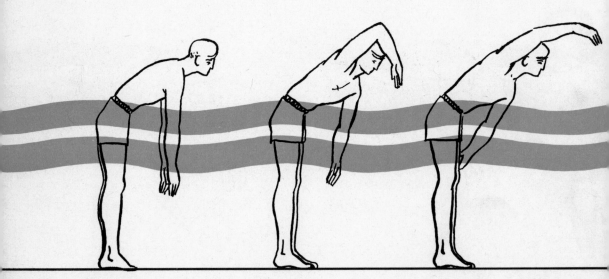

20

2. Lift your right shoulder and then your right elbow until it is as high as you can get it without turning around. Your forearm and hand should hang down loosely from the elbow.

3. From this high-elbow position, thrust your right hand and forearm straight forward, lifting your hand to shoulder level as you do. Hold the arm in that position while you perform Step Four.

4. Raise the left shoulder, then the elbow, then thrust forward with the hand and arm — at the same time bring the outstretched *right* hand and forearm down until it hangs in the original position. Your fingers should be slightly curled.

5. Now the left arm is outstretched. Repeat the lifting operation with the right arm, while lowering the left.

6. Continue this exercise until you get a feeling of rhythm. Do not hurry the movements. Stay relaxed and try to imagine — as you lower each arm — that it is pushing through water.

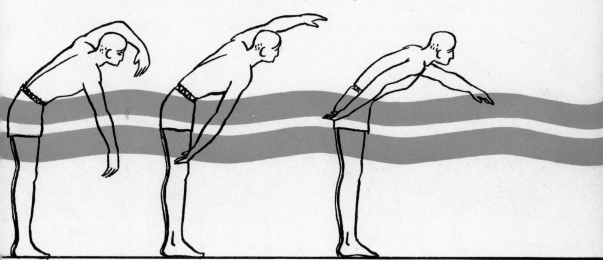

Now go into the water to a point where it is waist-high. Again bend forward just as you did on land, and practice the stroke, this time letting your arms go into the water. Feel how your cupped hands pull against the water on each stroke.

Now face in toward the shallow water and have your friend stand in front of you, about six feet away. Lean forward again, arms stretched out before you, and shove off with your feet as you did for the prone float. Meanwhile, have your friend swim on ahead of you.

Keeping your head above the water, start stroking and try to swim as far as your friend. On your second try, do everything exactly the same, but take a deep breath and stroke with your head down in the water.

After several tries with your head out of water, and several more with head under water, try using the flutter kick as you stroke and notice how this will move you a little faster through the water.

You are now swimming! But — you are not yet doing the crawl. Why? Because you must still learn to stroke, kick, and breathe

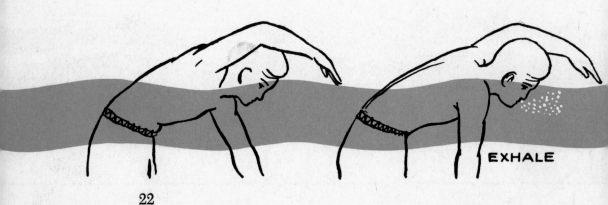

EXHALE

rhythmically — all at the same time. The first step in this lesson will again take place on the land.

Bend forward and start stroking, but now, as your left arm goes forward, turn your head to the right side and take a deep breath. As the right arm goes forward, bring your head back to a face-down position and let your breath out slowly.

Now stand in the water where it is a little above your waist. Lean forward just as you did before, but this time take a deep breath and put your face in the water. Your left arm should be extended and your right arm at your side. As your left arm strokes downward, and your right reaches forward to hit the water — exhale. Then, as you bring the left arm forward again, turn your head to the right, out of the water, and take a deep breath.

Practice this rhythmic breathing for a while, until you do it comfortably. Then face toward shallow water, shove off and start swimming toward your friend. Stroke with your arms, use the flutter kick, *inhale* with each left arm stroke, and *exhale* into the water with each right arm stroke.

If you make a mistake and inhale when you should exhale, getting a mouthful of water, spit the water out and stand up right away. Rest for a few minutes, then go back and try again.

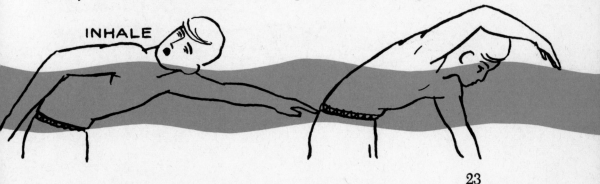

INHALE

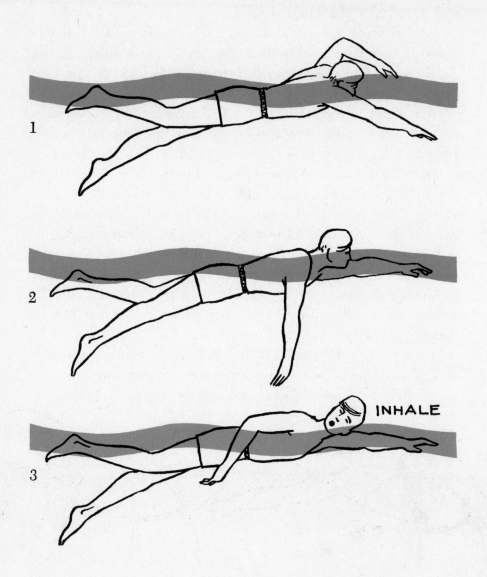

1

2

3 INHALE

24

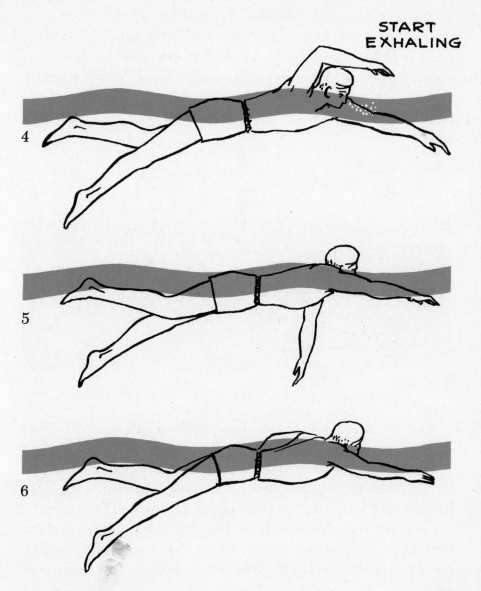

START
EXHALING

4

5

6

To increase the distance of your "solo" efforts (that means without any help) ask your friend to back up a little at a time, as you swim toward him. Then have him move sideward, so that you will have to turn as you swim. A turn is done by *shortening* the stroke on the side to which you are turning. In other words, if you want to turn to the right, then shorten the stroke of the right arm, and turn your head in that direction. Your body will follow.

Your breathing is now timed so that you will inhale once on each left stroke, and exhale on each right stroke.

What about the kick? This should also be timed, six beats of the legs to each two arm strokes (one left, one right). To learn this, the first lesson will be done up on the land again.

Lie down on a low bench so that your arms can hang down freely, and have room to stroke. As you bring each arm forward, count *one* as the arm begins to move, count *two* as the arm passes

over your head, and count *three* as it comes down in front of you (if you were swimming, the *three* would come as the arm hit the water). For *each* count kick once — first with the right leg, then with the left.

When you have made some progress in this, try to turn your head as the left arm goes forward. Use slow strokes at first, then increase the speed. When you think you have learned the timing of stroke, kick, and breathing, then try it in the water.

This six-beat kick is the one used by racing champions. It is not easily learned and you should not worry if your timing is a little off. Even champions make a mistake once in a while with it.

How far do you have to swim with the crawl before you can call yourself a swimmer? If you are learning in a pool, try to swim the width of the pool, that is, from side to side. This distance is usually about twenty-five feet. If you are in a lake or a pond, ask someone to stand about that distance away, and swim toward him, with your friend at your side.

When you can swim twenty-five feet by yourself, you are ready to try swimming a little in deep water. Start from shallow water and have your friend walk or swim beside you. Take short trips into the deeper water at first, than turn back.

The idea is to gain confidence in your ability to swim in water of any depth. As a final test, try to swim the length of the pool (from end to end), a distance usually of about twenty-five yards. If you are in a lake or a pond try to swim about the same distance. Your friend should stay nearby, and you should not try it until you feel sure you can do it.

The ability to swim a long way is called *endurance,* and this comes only with regular, correct practice. If you keep at your lessons and make sure you are doing everything right, it will not be long after your first "solo" before you are able to swim a good distance in either deep or shallow water.

Just how long it will take you to become a swimmer will depend on how much time you can spend on each lesson. Some learn faster than others, of course, but a dozen trips to the water is about average. If it should take you a few more than this, then you have had that much more practice.

Now let us discuss the other strokes used in swimming. You should try to learn these *only after* you can swim easily in deep water with the crawl. Use the same procedure with each of these new strokes that you used with the crawl, namely:

1.  Practice the stroke on land.
2.  Practice the stroke standing in waist-high water.
3.  Shove off and swim toward your friend.
4.  Shove off and swim by yourself, with your friend standing by.
5.  Use the stroke in deep water. (If you get tired while doing any of these new strokes, remember you can always switch over to the crawl.)

28

# The Backstroke

THERE are two kinds of backstrokes: a simple one used for informal swimming, and one used for racing.

In the *simple* backstroke, start with the back float position, both arms at your sides. Then draw both hands up along your sides to your armpits, extend them outward from your shoulders, then pull them back in a wide arc to your sides again.

The kick used with this stroke is different from the flutter kick. The legs draw up toward the body, knees pointing sideward and heels together. When they are drawn up tight, they are shoved back against the water, separating in a fast motion which ends with the legs fully extended and the feet about twelve inches apart. The heels are then brought together and you do the same thing all over again.

This is called the *frog* kick because it is copied from that familiar animal. The legs are drawn back at the same time that the hands are drawn up to the armpits and the arms are shot out to

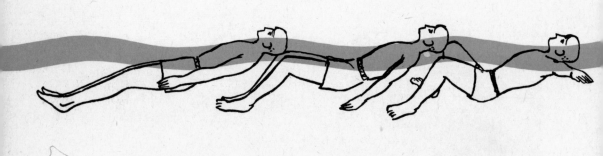

the side. The legs shove back as the arms pull forward through the water. Since your face is always out of the water there is no real breathing problem, but you will find it easiest with this stroke to inhale as the legs and arms are drawn up, then exhale as they pull and shove against the water.

Practice these movements on land, lying down. Do the arm-stroke first, then the frog kick, then the two together. To learn the timing, count *one* as the arms and legs are drawn up, count *two* as they shove back, then count *three* and *four* before starting the stroke again.

Go into the water, shove off backward and have your friend support you by the head, just as he did when you were learning the back float. After you have practiced for a while with his support, tell him to let go and try it on your own.

The simple backstroke is slow and relaxed. The counts of *three* and *four* allow you to glide through the water after each stroke, resting your arms and legs. This stroke can be used for a long time without tiring you, and it is a good one to use in case of emergency.

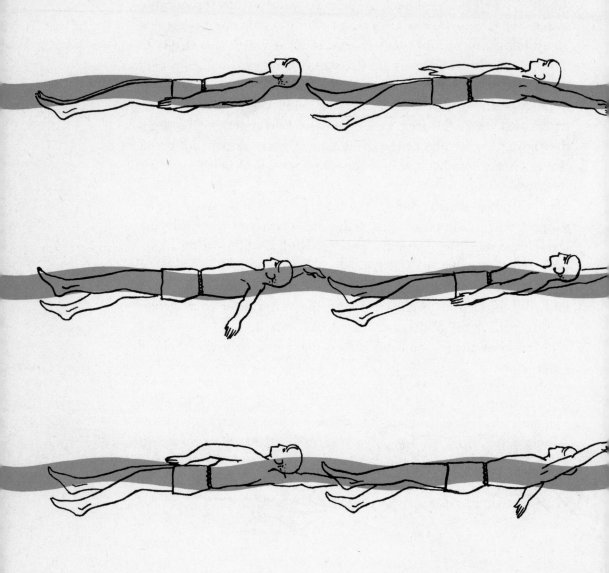

# The Racing Backstroke

THE RACING backstroke is really another version of the crawl, only this time you are lying on your back instead of your stomach.

You start with the back float again, both hands at your sides. Draw your left hand up along your side to your armpit, then continue to raise your arm until it is extended straight above your head. Twist your wrist away from your body so that the hand will enter the water palm-down. The fingers should be slightly curled. Then, with your arm still extended, pull your hand through the water and back to your side. Now do the same thing with your right arm.

The flutter kick is used with this stroke but with the feet, of course, now pointed upward. The legs are kept as close together as possible, and the toes are pointed forward so that the full surface of the foot will beat against the water on each kick. Again, a six-beat kick is used.

Follow the same order of practice as you did for the simple backstroke, except that, when you work on the land, lie on a low, narrow bench so that your arms can stroke freely on each side.

As your arm sweeps up over your head it should be kept relaxed, but the elbow may be bent sharply or slightly, whichever you prefer. It's a good idea to move your arm back as if you were reaching for something behind your head. Don't forget to twist your wrist and cup your palm.

Since your mouth is out of the water at all times, you may set your own breathing pattern. But it would be a good idea to stay with the rhythm of the crawl: inhale as your left arm goes back, exhale as the right arm goes back.

# The Breaststroke

To BEGIN the breaststroke, start with the prone float. Your hands should be just beneath the surface, held together at the chest — palms down. Sweep your hands forward, then out to the sides in a wide arc and then back to your sides. During this movement the arms should be fully extended from the shoulders. Then bring your hands up toward your chest, ready for the next stroke.

The kick used for the breaststroke is the frog kick. But instead of the arms and legs working together as they did in the simple backstroke, they now work at different times.

As the arms are brought up to the chest, the legs are drawn up to the body. Then, as the legs kick back, the arms shoot forward. When the arms pull back through the water, the legs are already fully extended.

34

After you have practiced the breaststroke in a standing position on land, lie down again on the bench and work on timing the stroke and the kick. Start from a position with the arms and legs fully extended and work to a count of four: *one* — arms pull back in the stroke; *two* — hands are brought to your chest and legs drawn up; *three* — hands shoot forward and legs kick back; *four* — heels are brought together and the arm stroke is started again.

Now go into the water and try the breaststroke, first with the arms working alone. Then try the frog kick alone (holding on to your friend's hands or the side of the pool for support of your upper body). Then try the two together. Start each time just as you would for the prone float, shoving off toward your friend. At all times, your head should be kept *above* the water. Inhale with each stroke of the arms, exhale with each kick of the legs.

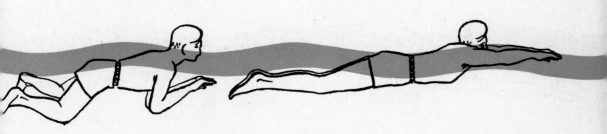

# The Sidestroke

THE SIDESTROKE is a slow, relaxed stroke, like the dog paddle and the simple backstroke. It lets the swimmer keep his head out of water at all times.

From a prone float position, roll over onto your right side. Extend your right arm up above your head and keep your left arm at your side. As the right hand pulls back through the water, the elbow bends so that the hand almost touches the shoulder. At the same time the left hand comes up to meet the right hand, the left elbow also bent. Then both arms return to their first position, the left hand pulling against the water, the right hand slipping overhead.

36

Several kicks may be used with the sidestroke. The two most popular are: 1. a modified form of the frog kick, with the legs being drawn up on the right-hand stroke and kicking back on the short left-hand stroke; 2. the *scissors* kick, with the legs being drawn up as in the frog kick, but on the kick-back they separate — the right leg going in front of the body and the left leg behind. Both legs are then quickly drawn together. It is this scissors motion, of course, that gives the kick its name.

Because of the body position, the sidestroke is hard to practice on land, except in a standing position. (Your right arm would be pinned under your body if you tried it lying down.) So, for land practice, do the arm stroke while standing, and do the kick while lying down.

TOP VIEW

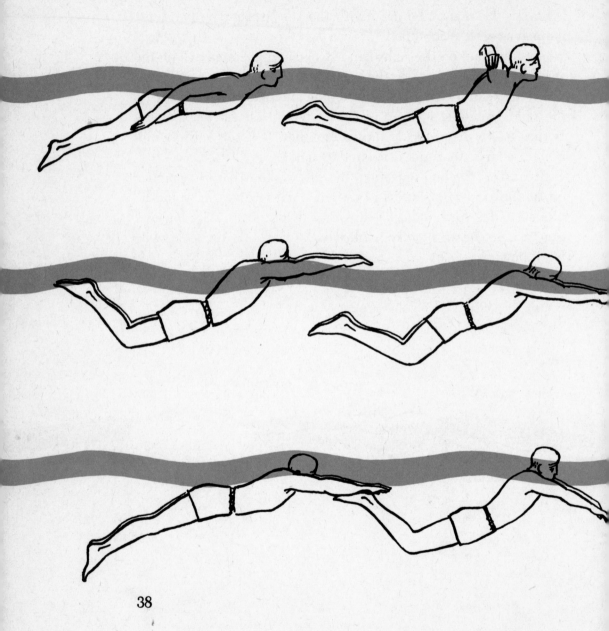

# The Butterfly Stroke

THIS STROKE is seldom used, except in racing. It is almost as fast as the crawl, but it is the most tiring of all strokes.

You start off as you did for the breaststroke, but with both arms back at your sides. Then both arms at once swing up and over your head and hit the water in front of you about a foot apart, palms facing down. They continue this wide arc down through the water, back to your sides, and then the movement is repeated.

Your body and head will bob up and down in the water with each stroke, rising as the arms pull back through the water, and sinking as the arms begin the stroke again. The legs are kept close together and, as the arms leave the water at the start of the stroke, the hips thrust upward, and the feet rise to the surface. When the arms pull through the water, the hips and feet come down.

This is called the *dolphin* kick because it resembles the motion of that graceful sea mammal. It's almost as if the lower half of the body were being cracked like a whip against the water.

When you practice the butterfly stroke on land, swing your arms freely. Reach them back as far as your muscles will allow

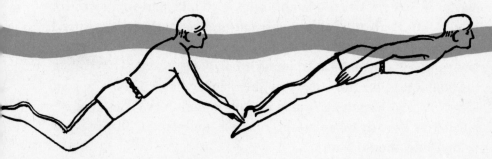

and, on the forward swing over your head, make sure the hands remain about a foot apart.

In the water, first practice the armstroke from a standing position. Then shove off and start swimming. Use only the armstroke at first. Then try the dolphin kick while holding onto your friend's hands. Then try both together. Notice how quickly your arms get tired with the butterfly stroke. It is a good idea to alternate a couple of these difficult butterfly strokes with a couple of the easier breaststrokes when you are first learning.

The butterfly can also be done with the frog kick. In this case, draw your legs up just as the arms finish their stroke through the water — as if your hands and feet were trying to touch. Kick as the arms are brought back through the air for the next stroke.

Whichever kick you use, the breathing rhythm is the same: inhale on the forward sweep of the arms, exhale on the stroke through the water, while your face is under the surface.

## Now You Must Practice

THESE are just about all the strokes you will have to learn to become a good swimmer. You must practice each one before you can master it. Except when you are training to take part in a race, you should think about building up *endurance*, rather than speed. And the best way to build up endurance is by doing each stroke over and over again — and doing it *correctly*.

Soon after you have learned the strokes, it would be a good idea to take a lifesaving course in your community. These courses teach you how to take care of yourself, and others, in the water if anything should happen.

40

INHALE

LEGS SPLIT

41

# Simple Diving

ABOUT the only thing common to swimming and diving is that both are connected with the water. Even then, there is a difference, for swimming is done in the water while the main part of diving takes place before you hit the water.

In this book, however, we are going to discuss only poolside, or simple diving, and the racing dive. Fancy diving, from springboards and platforms, is another sport that requires special training.

While swimming can be learned in any body of shallow water, diving should be learned only where the water is still, preferably a pool, which provides safe takeoff areas for the beginner, or a still-water pond. Even when you have learned how to dive, never dive into a lake or pond without first finding out what is under the water.

The first step is to feel what it is like to enter the water *suddenly*. While you were learning to swim, the rule was to enter the water gradually at all times. But now you must find out what it is like to hit the water all at once.

Stand at poolside and jump down into the deep water, taking a deep breath just before you go. If your feet hit bottom, just give a shove to return to the surface, or, work your arms down against the water and you'll soon bob up again. Try this "jumping dive" a few times.

Now you are ready to enter the water head first. Crouch down at the side of the pool, toes gripping the edge, arms wrapped around your legs and chin almost touching the tops of your knees.

From this position, take a deep breath and simply fall forward

43

into the water with your eyes closed. Hold on to your legs until your body is all the way under water. Then let go, unbend and stroke with your arms to rise to the surface. Try this a few more times, and you will have overcome one of the big problems in learning to dive: going into the water head first.

Two big steps remain: to get your body to follow your head in a straight line, and finally, to get the legs to follow the head and body.

Squat at poolside, trunk fully erect and arms extended straight from the shoulders. Duck your head between your arms, take a deep breath and fall forward into the pool. Your arms, head, and body should be in a straight line as your hands hit the water. Knees should not leave the ground until pulled off by the weight

of your falling body. Try this several times, making sure that your head stays down all the way into the water.

When you can perform this knee dive smoothly, you are ready to try your first standing dive. Take the same position with your arms as in the knee dive, but this time stand up. Bend forward so that your arms are pointing at the water, take a deep breath, duck your head between your arms and fall forward. What happened? Did you hit the water belly first? Nearly everyone does, the first time.

A good diving rule is to follow a failure with another try. But let's take a moment to see what went wrong. Probably your legs caused the bad dive, for you did all right in the knee dive, when your legs couldn't spoil things. Most likely you bent your knees as you fell forward and your feet left the ground too soon.

On your second try make sure your knees do not bend and your feet do not leave the ground before your falling body actually

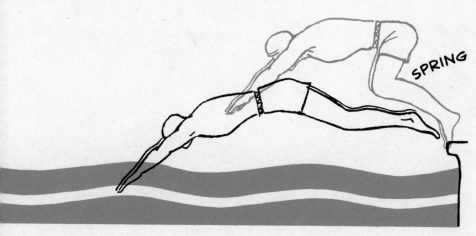

SPRING

pulls them off. What? Another belly flop? Maybe this time you forgot to keep your head down.

It may take you a day or two before arms, head, body, and legs fall properly into line. The main thing is not to get discouraged — don't be too serious about it, and don't try too hard. Set a certain number of tries a day — say three sets of three dives each — separated by some swimming. Before you know it, you will be diving!

Once you have mastered this falling-in dive, it's time to get those legs of yours to do some of the work. As you fall toward the water from a standing position, shove upward with your feet when you are about halfway to the water. You will find, after a few failures, that your legs reach their proper position easier with this shove. Soon you can stop the falling method, and try a real "front dive," using more leg spring.

For this front dive, stand erect at poolside, arms at your sides. On the take-off, crouch down slightly for more leg spring. Swing your arms forward and shove off, remembering to keep your head down. On all dives don't forget the deep breath before take-off.

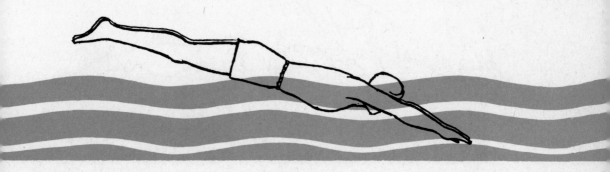

# The Racing Dive

EVERY swimming race, except one — the backstroke — begins with a dive. This is called a *racing* dive and is a streamlined, non-painful version of our old friend, the belly flop.

The purpose of the racing dive is to get you into the water fast and in position to start swimming. So you try to skim along the top of the water, your whole body hitting at almost the same time, in order not to sink down too much and be slowed up.

The racing dive is done from the deep end of the pool, but not from the diving board — that would give you a big head start! Take your position at the very edge of the pool, toes curled around the rim, knees bent, body crouched. The arms should swing slightly and hang down from the shoulders. The head should be up and eyes fixed on the far end of the pool.

Someone gives the command, "On your mark!" and you get ready to shove off. When you hear "Go!" you dive.

The proper form of the racing dive is to hit the water with arms straight forward, head lowered between them, stomach sucked in, and the body in a straight line from the tips of your fingers to the tips of your toes. To do this you must — at the word "Go!" — swing your arms forward fast and push off hard *over* the water. Remember, do not aim *down into* the water, for then you will sink too deep and lose time. Your body should reach the outstretched, full-length position a split second before you hit the water.

Once in the water, you will sink slightly beneath the surface. Start kicking your legs — using whichever kick fits the stroke you are swimming — but don't stroke with your arms until just before you come up. The pull of the first stroke should be completed just as your head comes above the water. If you stroke too soon, your arms will slow the good start the dive gave you; if you start too late, you will slow down and valuable seconds will be lost.

It will take a lot of practice before you learn the racing dive perfectly. In fact, many champion swimmers still have trouble with it. But it is worth all the practice time spent on it, because in the shorter races, a good dive can make all the difference between winning and losing.

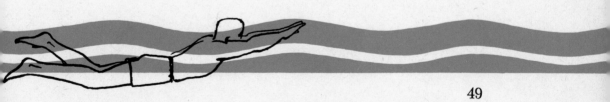

# Why Not Be a Racing Swimmer?

You CAN BEGIN to swim in races almost as soon as you are old enough to go to school. There is a regular program of events — called the Junior Olympics — for boys and girls as young as nine, and informal races, are held at even earlier ages.

These racing *meets* are the same in many ways as those held for high school and college swimmers. One difference is that the distances are shorter. Junior swimmers (those below the high school level) are limited to twenty-five yards, or, at the most, fifty yards. But the strokes are the same as for high school and college: crawl, breaststroke, backstroke, and butterfly.

Swimming meets are held in pools of different sizes. The accepted length for indoor pools is twenty or twenty-five yards, with twenty-five tending to be the favorite. Outdoor pools — used mainly for the Olympic Games and national championships — are either fifty yards or fifty meters (about fifty-five yards). Separate records are kept for each size pool.

Short pools produce faster timing than long pools because they require more laps (lengths) for each race and therefore more turns. When a swimmer pushes off from the end wall of the pool with his legs on each turn, he travels faster than the fastest swimming stroke could carry him, for about four or five yards. Let's see how he does it.

*Racers swim in lanes*

All pools used for racing are divided into *lanes*, marked by stripes painted on the bottom of the pool, and sometimes by ropes on top of the water. Each lane is about seven feet wide. The line

50

on the bottom marks the center of the lane and is a guide to the
swimmer during the race.

A swimmer must stay in his own lane or risk being *disqualified*
(put out of the race). It is hard, at first, to keep to a straight
course — particularly in the backstroke, where the swimmer has
no guide except his sense of direction. But with practice you will
develop the knack for this.

### The men in charge of meets

Swimming meets require more officials than a basketball or
baseball game. There is a *starter,* who gets the swimmers off their
marks; *judges* pick the order of the finish, and *timers* clock the
swimmers. In championship meets there are two judges and three
timers for *each lane.* There is also the *referee,* who makes sure the
.rules are obeyed, and settles conflicting decisions of the judges.

51

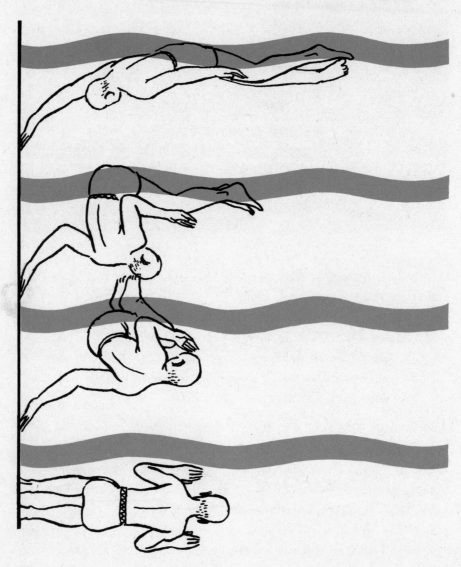

## The racing turn

According to the rules of swimming a racer must touch the end of the pool with one or both hands as he completes each lap and before starting his turn. An exception is made for junior and high school free-style races, but even here he should be at least close enough to touch the end before making the turn, otherwise he may miss the end wall of the pool with his feet.

Once the touch is made, the swimmer does a half-somersault, with a half-twist under water, bringing his feet into position against the end wall of the pool for the shove-off. The somersault and twist should be completed before the shove-off, so that the swimmer receives the full power supplied by his uncoiling legs.

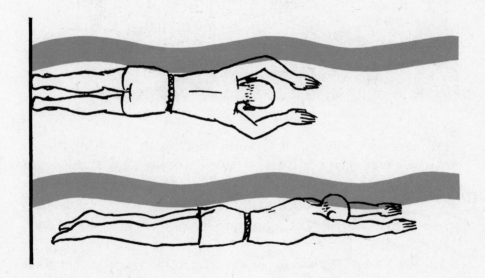

# How a Swimming Meet Is Run

THE OBJECT of a swimming race is very simple — to get from start to finish ahead of the other swimmers, while obeying the rules for your event. The judges pick the racers as they hit the finish line. When there are too many swimmers in a race to fit into a pool at one time, *heats* (preliminary races) are held and the fastest swimmers are chosen to take part in the final race later in the day.

*How a race is started*

All races except the backstroke start with a racing dive. Swimmers take their positions by the edge of the pool, at the deep end. The starter says, "On your marks!" and the swimmers crouch tensely, knees slightly bent, ready for the dive. At the command "Go!" or the firing of a blank pistol, they are off their marks and into the water.

For the backstroke, the swimmers go into the water at the deep end. They take a firm grip with their hands on the gutter which runs along all four sides of the pool, just under the edge. Both feet are planted firmly against the end wall of the pool under water. The legs are doubled up so that the knees almost touch the chin. At the command, "On your marks!" they raise their bodies up slightly, ready to shove off when the pistol fires.

Should the starter feel that a contestant in any race has "beaten the gun," he will fire a second shot to recall the swimmers and then start them again. College rules call for a swimmer to be disqualified after three "false starts."

## How a race ends

A racer completes a race when he swims the required number of laps and his hands have touched the end of the pool at the finish. In the breaststroke and the butterfly *both* hands must touch at the same time. The timers start their clocks when the pistol flashes; they stop them when the swimmer has completed his course.

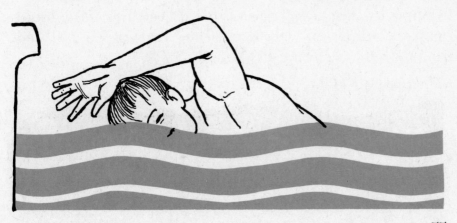

# The Events in a Swimming Meet

A SWIMMING meet has no innings like a baseball game nor is it divided into quarters like a football game. It is made up, instead, of a certain number of *events*, scheduled in advance by the men who are running the meet.

In junior meets, these men — together, they are called a committee — decide how many races they will include. In doing this, they are guided by the list of events in the Junior Olympic program of the Amateur Athletic Union (A.A.U.). In high school and college competition there is a set program of events which must be followed. The same is true for open A.A.U. meets and the Olympic games.

The events in high school are: 50-yard, 100-yard, and 200-yard free-style; 100-yard backstroke; 100-yard breaststroke; 100-yard butterfly; 150-yard individual medley; 200-yard free-style relay; 200-yard medley relay.

Colleges have a similar program, with the addition of longer free-style races, such as the 440-yard, 800-yard, and 1500 meters (a little less than a mile) races. The college backstroke, breaststroke, butterfly, and individual medley distances are 200 yards and the relay events are at 400 yards.

*The free-style event*

As the name implies, any stroke may be use in a free-style race. But, almost without exception, free-style racers use the crawl.

56

When the first organized swimming races were held, late in the nineteenth century, all races were free-style events. England was the birthplace of the sport and the English swimmers first used a type of breaststroke. It was an Australian who first introduced the crawl, probably copied from the East Indian natives.

The "Australian crawl" has been improved over the past fifty years, chiefly by Americans, and the version now used in races is called the "American crawl." It is the one described in this book.

Since there is freedom of choice in a free-style event, there are few rules to think about. A swimmer may even touch bottom with his feet during the race, for instance, so long as he does not advance by walking.

*The backstroke event*

Either the racing, or the simple backstroke may be used in this event, but the first is preferred, since it is a much faster stroke. The swimmer must stay on his back throughout the race, and must touch the end of the pool with his outstretched hand before going into a racing turn.

*The breaststroke event*

The arms in the breaststroke must work together and some part of the head must always be above the surface, except on the first stroke after the racing dive, and on the first stroke after each turn. The body must rest flat on the chest, shoulders in line with the surface of the water.

Hands must be pushed forward together from the chest, on or under the surface of the water (but never above the water). The hands should be brought back together and neither one should be allowed to get ahead of the other. The legs should use only the frog kick and must also work together. Any sidestroke motion of the arms, or the use of the dolphin kick, disqualifies the swimmer.

*The butterfly event*

Until a few years ago, the butterfly stroke was allowed in the breaststroke event. When the dolphin kick was developed, the butterfly became a separate event. In this race, the arms must leave the water on each stroke, must work together, and the shoulders must be kept in line with the surface of the water.

Swimmers may use the frog kick in the butterfly, although more speed can usually be generated with the dolphin. Most junior swimmers use the frog kick because they find it impossible to use the dolphin kick for long.

*The individual medley event*

In a medley race, the swimmers use three or four different strokes in turn, each for the same distance. High school swimmers do fifty yards of butterfly, fifty yards of backstroke, and fifty yards of free-style, in that order. College swimmers add fifty yards of breaststroke between the backstroke and the free-style.

These strokes are done one after another, without rest, so that the medley is a test of endurance as well as all-round ability. The same rules are in force for each of the strokes as in the individual events just described.

*The relays*

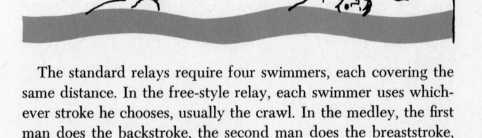

The standard relays require four swimmers, each covering the same distance. In the free-style relay, each swimmer uses whichever stroke he chooses, usually the crawl. In the medley, the first man does the backstroke, the second man does the breaststroke, the third man does the butterfly, and the fourth man does the crawl.

Relay swimmers have no stick to hand to the next man, as in a track meet, so each man must wait until his teammate has completed his distance before he shoves off. All the swimmers, except those doing the backstroke in the medley relay, start with a racing dive. An official holds the swimmer's leg, and lets go when it is time for him to dive. If he starts before the official lets go, the team is disqualified.

# How to Score a Meet

SWIMMING is a team sport as well as an individual sport. The swimmers earn points for their teams according to their finish, and these points are totaled to decide which team has won the meet. Scoring is done according to how many teams are in a meet, and also according to how many lanes are available in a championship meet.

The chart below will show you how the scoring is handled for all types of meets.

| Type of Meet | Scoring | | | | | | | |
|---|---|---|---|---|---|---|---|---|
| | 1st | 2nd | 3rd | 4th | 5th | 6th | 7th | 8th |
| Dual Meet (two teams) | 5 | 3 | 1 | 0 | 0 | 0 | 0 | 0 |
| 4-lane meet | 5 | 3 | 2 | 1 | 0 | 0 | 0 | 0 |
| 4-lane relay | 10 | 6 | 4 | 2 | 0 | 0 | 0 | 0 |
| 5-lane meet | 6 | 4 | 3 | 2 | 1 | 0 | 0 | 0 |
| 5-lane relay | 12 | 8 | 6 | 4 | 2 | 0 | 0 | 0 |
| 6-lane meet | 7 | 5 | 4 | 3 | 2 | 1 | 0 | 0 |
| 6-lane relay | 14 | 10 | 8 | 6 | 4 | 2 | 0 | 0 |

For all meets of more than six lanes, the 6-lane scoring system is used.

# A Final Word

UNLIKE many sports, young people as well as grownups can take part in national swimming championships, and even in world championships. Teenage swimmers, for example, dominated the Olympic games at Melbourne, Australia, and they hold most of the world records.

But this does not mean that the road to becoming a swimming champion is an easy one. As in any sport, many hours of practice are necessary to reach championship form — even if you start with championship ability. All racing swimmers must observe a strict diet and they usually stay in training all year round. Real racing, however, is generally limited to the winter and summer months.

A great swimmer must develop both his stroke and his kick. Thus, in practicing, you should do several laps of the pool *using only your arms,* then several more *using only your legs.* Practice your racing dive and learn to pace yourself for longer races. Try racing with each of the strokes to find out which you do best — then concentrate on that one.

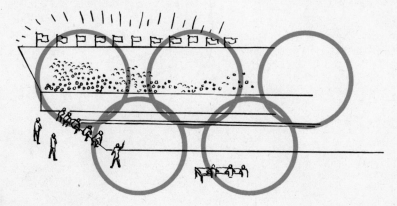

# Index

A.A.U. *see* Amateur Athletic Union
Amateur Athletic Union, 56
American crawl, 57
   *see also* Crawl stroke
Arms, 16
   backstroke, 30-31
   breaststroke, 34-35
   butterfly stroke, 39-40
   crawl stroke, 20-21
   diving, 42-49
   dog paddle, 19
   floating, 9, 10, 13
   kicking, 14, 16
   racing backstroke, 33
   side stroke, 36-37
   treading water, 17
Australia, 61
Australian crawl, 57

Back float, 9, 11-13, 14, 33
Backstroke event, 57
Backstrokes, 30-31, 33, 50, 51, 59
   in swimming race, 48-54
Beaches, 3, 4
"Beating the gun," 55
Belly flop, 45, 46, 47, 48
Breaststroke, 34-35, 40, 50, 55, 59
Breaststroke event, 57-58
Breath control, 1, 6-8, 10, 14-15, 22-23,
     26, 31, 33, 42, 45
   in basin, 7
Buoyancy, 9
Butterfly event, 58
Butterfly stroke, 38-40, 50, 55, 59

Chill, 3

College events, 56
College meets, 56
Committee, 56
Confidence, 28
Contestants, 55
Cramps, 2
Crawl stroke, 20-27, 48, 57, 59

Diet, 61
Diving, 42-49
Diving board, 48
Disqualifications, 51, 55, 58
Dog paddle, 19-19, 36
Dolphin kick, 38, 39, 58
Dunking, 3

East Indian natives, 57
Endurance, 28, 40
England, 57
Events, 56-59

Face *see* Breath control
Falling-in dives, 42, 44, 45, 47
"False starts," 55
Fancy diving, 42
Fingers, 19, 20, 21, 33
Finish line, 54
Floating, 1, 6, 9-13
Flutter kick, 14-15, 22, 23
Food, 2, 61
Free-style events, 56-57
Free-style relays, 59
Free-style stroke, 56-57
Frog kick, 30-31, 34, 35, 58
   modified, 37
Front dive, 47

Hands *see* Arms
Heats, 54
High school events, 56
High school meets, 56
High school swimmer, 50, 58

Indoor pools, 50
Instructors, aid from, 14, 22, 26, 27, 31, 35

Judges, 51, 54
Jumping dive, 42
Junior Olympics, 50, 56
Junior meets, 56

Kicking, 1, 6, 14-15, 61
   after racing dive, 49
   backstroke, 30-31
   breaststroke, 34-35
   butterfly stroke, 39-40
   crawl stroke, 22, 27
   dog paddle, 18-19
   racing backstroke, 33
   sidestroke, 36
Knee dive, 44-45
Knees *see* Kicking *and* Legs

Lakes 3, 4, 5, 27, 28
Lanes, 51, 60
Laps, 48, 49, 53
Legs, 9, 17 *see also* Kicking
Lengths *see* Laps
Lifeguards, 3
Life saving course, 40

Medley race, 58-59
Meets, 50-51, 54-60
   disqualifications, 51, 55, 58
   events, 56-59
   heats, 54
   officials, 51
   scoring, 60

starts, 54-55
Melbourne, 61
Mouth *see* Breath control
Muscles, 2, 9

National championships, 50
Nose, 6
   *see also* Breath control

Ocean beaches, 3, 4
Olympic Games, 50, 56, 61
Organized racing, 1
   *see also* Meets
Outdoor pools, 50

Points *see* Scoring
Ponds, 4, 27, 28
Pools, 3, 5, 27, 28, 42, 48
   gutter, 54
   regulation sizes, 50
Poolside diving, 42-49
Practice, 40, 61
   *see also* Training
Preliminary races *see* Heats
Prone float, 9-11, 14, 22, 34

Racing *see* Meets
Racing backstroke, 33, 57
Racing dive, 42, 48-49, 54
Racing meets, 50
   *see also* Meets
Racing swimmer, 49-50
Racing turns, 50
Referees, 51
Relays, 59
Rescuer, 3

Safety rules, 2-3
Scissors kick, 37
Scoring, 60
Shove-off, 53
"Show off," 3

Sidestroke, 36-37, 58
Simple backstroke, 30-31, 36, 57
Simple diving, 42-47
Six-beat kick, 26-27, 33
"Solo" swimming, 26, 28
Somersaults, 53
Springboards, 42
Standing dive, 45, 47
Starters, 51, 54, 55
Still-water pond, 42
Strokes, 1, 28
    see under type of stroke
Stroking, 6, 16
    see also Arms
Swimmers:
    beginners, 1-5
    experts, 6, 49
Swimming, dangers of, 2, 3
Swimming meets, 50
    see also Meets
Swimming pool, 4
    see also Pools

Swimming race, 48
    see Meets

Take off areas, 42
Teams, scoring of, 60
Thunderstorms, 2
Timers, 51, 55
Touches, 57
Training, 28, 39, 61
Treading water, 17, 18
Turns, 26, 53, 57
Twists, 53

Water:
    deep, 17
    entering, 5, 42
    "feel" of, 5
    horseplay in, 3
    obstructions, 4, 42
    shallow, 42
Water safety, 1-3